Edwina Riddell studied graphic design at the London College of Printing and worked for ten years as a freelance illustrator. Now, with two small children, her major interest is in children's books. She has illustrated **Outside-in** and **See How You Grow**, both of which are lift-the -flap body books. **100 First Words** is the first in the series of "My first" books.

For Helen

100 First Words © Frances Lincoln Limited 1988
Illustrations copyright © Edwina Riddell 1988

100 First Words was conceived, edited and designed by Frances Lincoln Limited,
4 Torriano Mews, Torriano Avenue, London NW5 2RZ

British Library Cataloguing in Publication Data available on request

ISBN 0-7112-0513-2 hardback
ISBN 0-7112-0512-4 paperback

Printed in Hong Kong

15 17 19 18 16 14

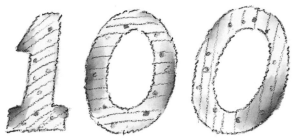

100

first words

to say with your baby

Edwina Riddell

FRANCES
LINCOLN

Granny

Mummy

baby

Daddy

boy

Grandad

girl

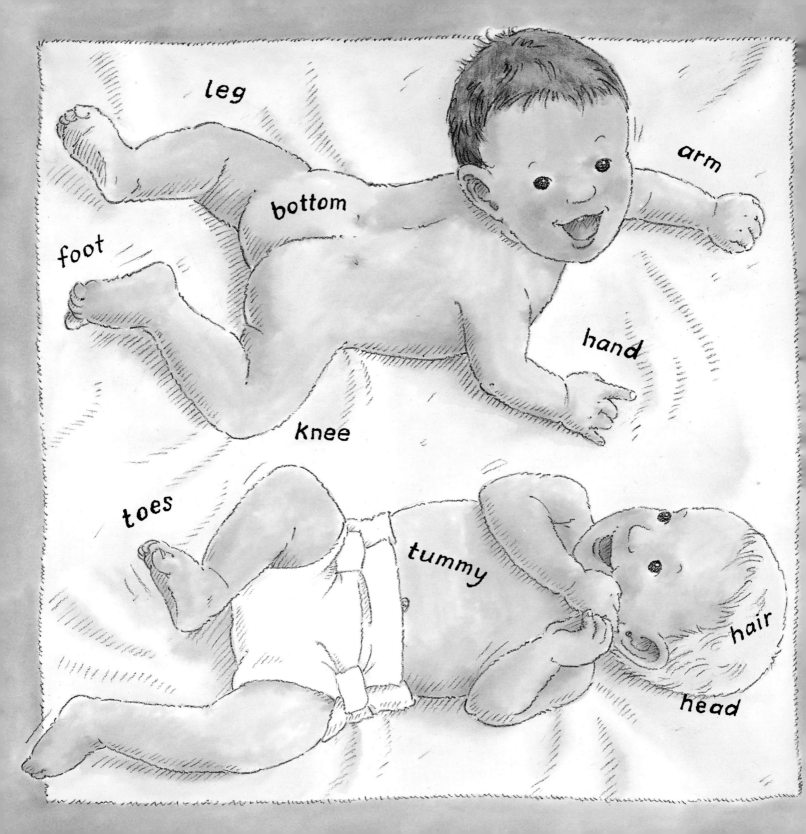

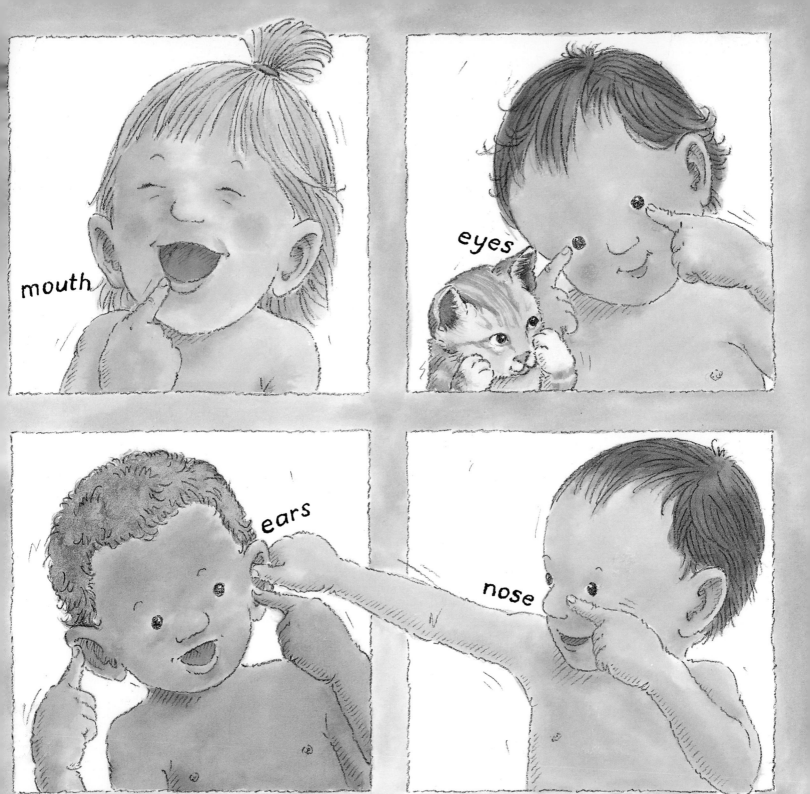

mouth

eyes

ears

nose

jacket

dungarees

gloves

shoes

boots

jumper

pants

hat

vest

socks

nappy

dress

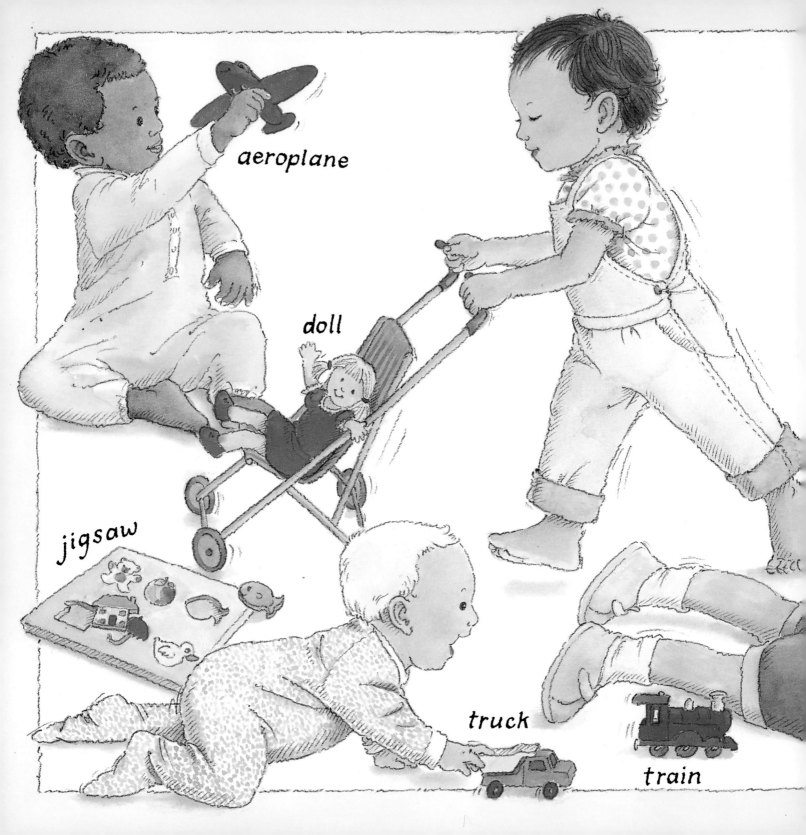

aeroplane

doll

jigsaw

truck

train

bricks

tricycle

crayon

paper

phone

sunhat

Sand

bucket

spade

Shells

car

window

carseat

door

wheel

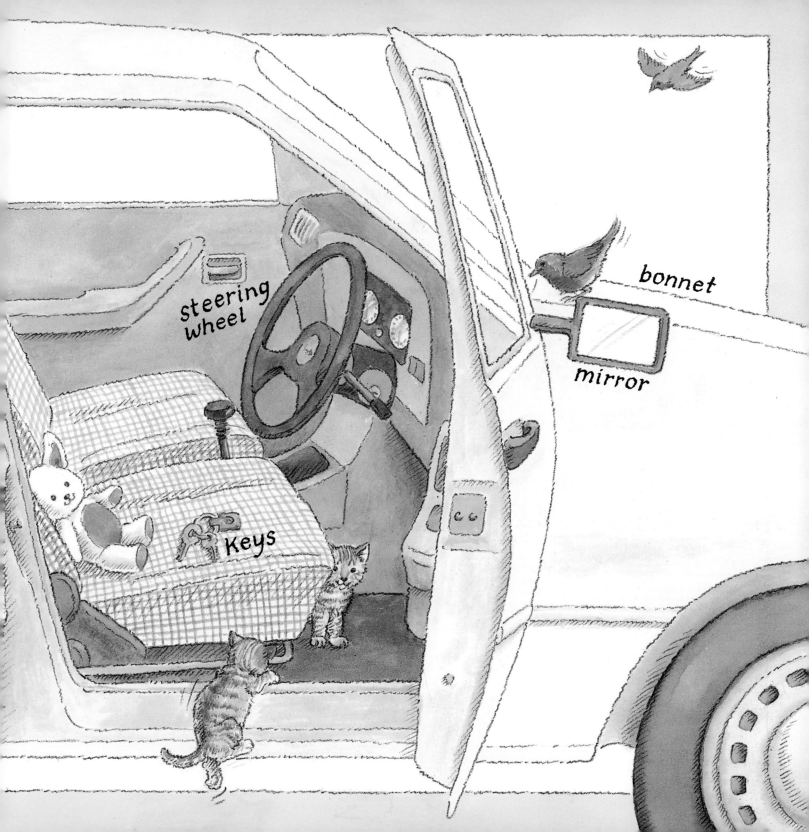

steering wheel

bonnet

mirror

Keys

shelves

bread

trolley

bottle

till

packet

tins

eggs

box

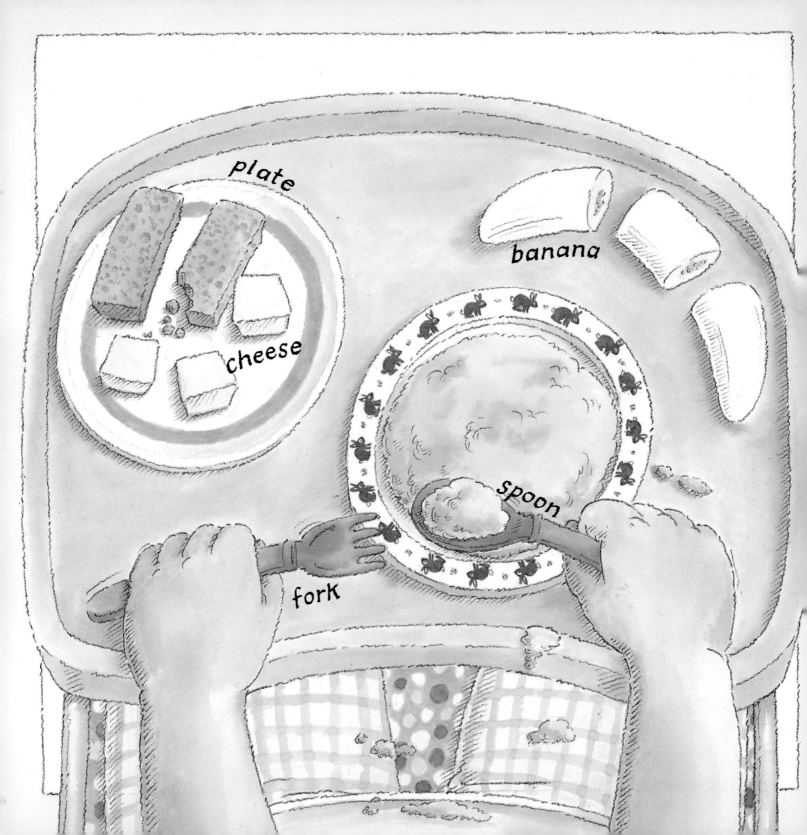

highchair

bib

cup

bottle

bowl

bird

swing

butterfly

buggy

leaves

duck

squirrel

flowers

grass

dog

kitten

budgies

fish

cat

rabbits

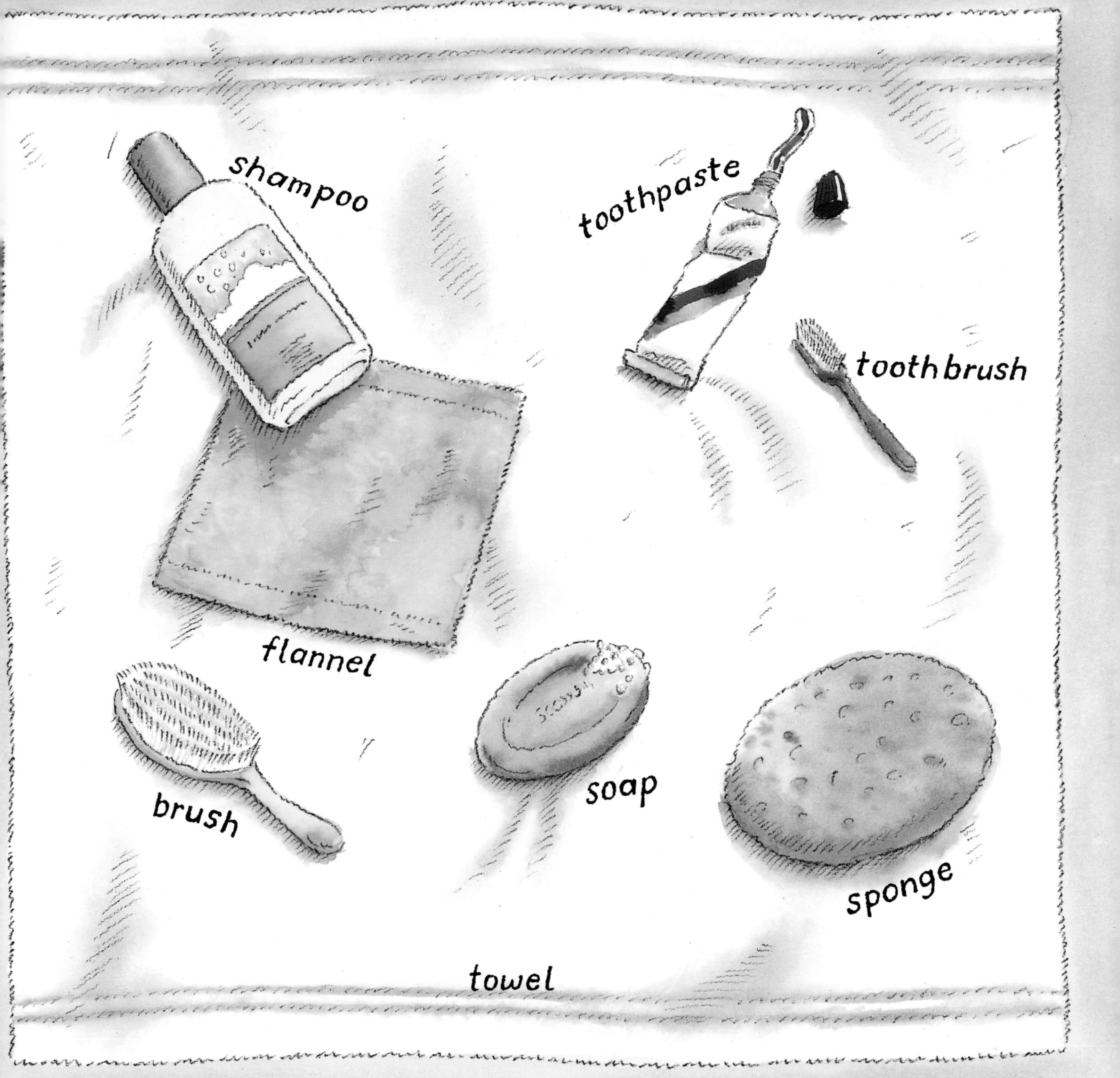

shampoo

toothpaste

toothbrush

flannel

brush

soap

sponge

towel

mobile

light

cot

teddy

book

clock

pyjamas

blanket

pillow

duvet

bed